A BIOGRAPHY

GERONIMO

MARK L. GARDNER

WESTERN NATIONAL PARKS ASSOCIATION | TUCSON, ARIZONA

CONTENTS

APACHE

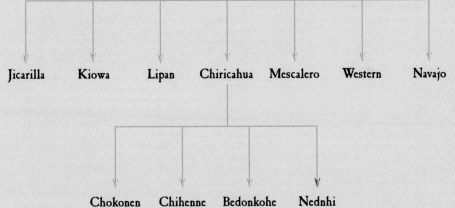

Jicarilla   Kiowa   Lipan   Chiricahua   Mescalero   Western   Navajo

Chokonen   Chihenne   Bedonkohe   Nednhi

THE LIFE & TIMES OF

GERONIMO

Circa 1825
Geronimo (*Goyahkla*) born near the headwaters of the
Gila River in present-day New Mexico.

January 20, 1851	March 3, 1851	October 12, 1872	April 21, 1877	August 2, 1878	September, 1881	February, 1884
Geronimo gains renown in a fight with Mexican troops at Pozo Hediondo (now Gran Esperanza), Sonora.	Geronimo's mother, wife, and three children killed by Mexican force at Janos, Chihuahua.	Chiricahua leader Cochise enters treaty with the United States, creating a separate reservation for the Chiricahua in the southeast corner of Arizona. The reservation is revoked in 1876.	Geronimo and his followers arrested at the Ojo Caliente Reservation, New Mexico. They are taken to the San Carlos Reservation in Arizona.	Geronimo and family flee San Carlos. Geronimo returns to the reservation in December 1879 or January 1880.	Geronimo again breaks out of the San Carlos Reservation. He and other renegade Chiricahua are tracked down in Mexico by U.S. troops and Apache scouts under Gen. George Crook in May 1883.	Geronimo and thirty-one followers return to San Carlos.

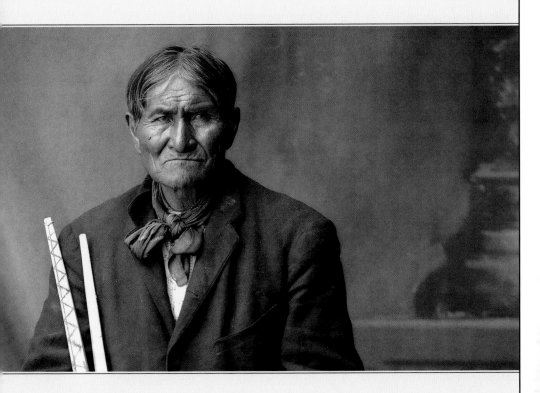

May, 1885
Geronimo leaves the San Carlos Reservation for the last time; takes refuge across the border in Mexico.

March 25–27, 1886
Council between General Crook and Geronimo at Cañon de los Embudos, Mexico. Geronimo agrees to return to San Carlos but slips away with forty-six other Chiricahua on the night of the 28th.

September 4, 1886
Geronimo surrenders to Gen. Nelson A. Miles at Skeleton Canyon. Geronimo and his men are incarcerated at Fort Pickens, Florida.

1888
Geronimo and surviving members of the Chiricahua tribe congregate at Mount Vernon Barracks, Alabama.

September 18, 1894
Chappo Geronimo, son of Geronimo, dies in Geronimo's arms at Mount Vernon Barracks. The Chiricahua are removed to Fort Sill, Oklahoma, that fall.

September, 1906
Geronimo's dictated memoirs published under the title *Geronimo's Story of His Life*.

February 17, 1909
Geronimo dies at Fort Sill, Oklahoma. One newspaper runs the headline "A Good Indian At Last."

FORT BOWIE NATIONAL HISTORIC SITE

I am old now and shall never
go on the warpath again, but if
I were young, and followed the
warpath, it would lead
into Old Mexico.

—GERONIMO, 1906

He had at least eight wounds in his leathered body of eighty-plus years: "shot in the right leg above the knee, and still carry the bullet; shot through the left forearm; wounded in the right leg below the knee with a saber; wounded on top of the head with the butt of a musket; shot just below the outer corner of the left eye; shot in left side; shot in the back." At one time he had been the most feared Indian on the North American continent. He did not hesitate to disburse death to man, woman, and child alike. Yet for an artist painting Geronimo's portrait at Fort Sill, Oklahoma, the old warrior, medicine man, and prisoner of war sang songs. "He had a deep, rich voice," remembered artist E. A. Burbank, "and these songs, sung in the Apache dialect, were of great beauty." This is the song of Geronimo, Chiricahua Apache:

O, ha le
O, ha le
Through the air
I fly upon a cloud
Toward the sky, far, far, far,
O, ha le
O, ha le
There to find the holy place
Ah, now the change comes o'er me!
O, ha le
O, ha le

APACHERÍA

Geronimo and his Chiricahua lived primarily in southeastern Arizona and southwestern New Mexico, but their raiding and trading forays took them deep into Sonora and Chihuahua, Mexico. Known as *Apachería,* this entire region comprised several thousand square miles, shared and contested by other Apache groups, Hispanos, and Anglos. Geronimo and his followers knew its mesas, canyons, mountain ranges, rivers, and deserts as only those who had lived and died there for generations could.

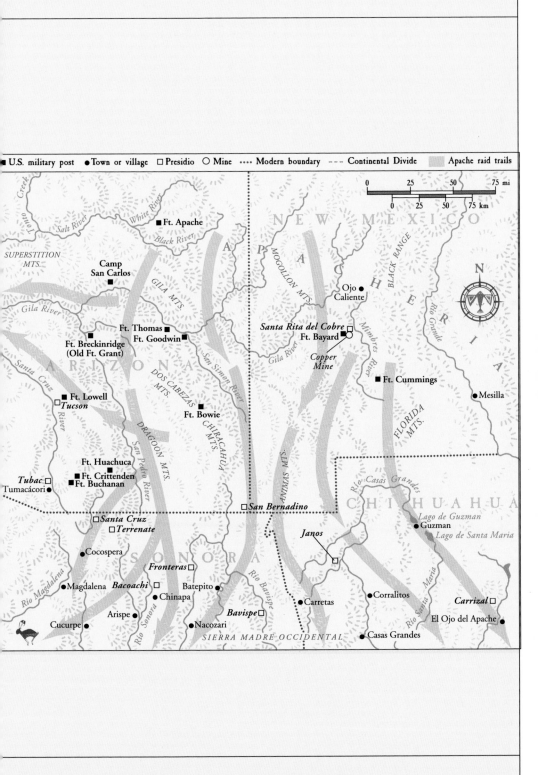

■ U.S. military post   ● Town or village   □ Presidio   ○ Mine   ···· Modern boundary   --- Continental Divide   ▓ Apache raid trails

0   25   50   75 mi
0   25   50   75 km

N

SUPERSTITION MTS.

NEW MEXICO

A P A C H E R I A

■ Ft. Apache

Black River

White River

Salt River

Tonto Creek

■ Camp San Carlos

Gila River

Gila MTS.

MOGOLLON MTS.

BLACK RANGE

Ojo ● Caliente

Rio Grande

Santa Rita del Cobre □ ○
Ft. Bayard ■ ○

■ Ft. Thomas
■ Ft. Goodwin

Copper Mine

Gila River

Mimbres River

■ Ft. Breckinridge
(Old Ft. Grant)

A R I Z O N A

DOS CABEZAS MTS.

San Simon River

■ Ft. Cummings

● Mesilla

Santa Cruz River

■ Ft. Lowell
□ *Tucson*

■ Ft. Bowie

CHIRACAHUA MTS.

FLORIDA MTS.

DRAGOON MTS.

San Pedro River

■ Ft. Huachuca
■ Ft. Crittenden
■ Ft. Buchanan

Tubac □
Tumacácori ●

ANIMAS MTS.

□ *San Bernadino*

C H I H U A H U A

Rio Casas Grandes

···· □ *Santa Cruz*
□ *Terrenate*

Lago de Guzman
● Guzman
Lago de Santa Maria

Janos ●

□

● Cocospera

S O N O R A

Fronteras □

● Magdalena   *Bacoachi* □   ● Batepito

Rio Casas Grandes

● Corralitos

Carrizal □

Rio Magdalena

● Chinapa

Rio Bavispe

● Carretas

Rio Santa Maria

● El Ojo del Apache

● Arispe

Bavispe □

Rio Sonora

● Cucurpe

● Nacozari

SIERRA MADRE OCCIDENTAL

● Casas Grandes

THE APACHE

The Apaches are born and reared in the open air of
the country, and fortified by simple foods, are
possessed of amazing hardiness.

—LT. JOSÉ CORTÉS, 1799

YUCCA AND BEAR GRASS AMID WATER-SCULPTED BOULDERS, COCHISE STRONGHOLD, ARIZONA

In history and legend, the Apache, or *Indeh* in their own language, have long been associated with the arid Southwest, primarily the mountains, deserts, and canyonlands of present-day Arizona, New Mexico, and northern Mexico. Centuries ago, however, this Athapaskan-speaking people were found far to the north in what is now Canada. At some point, probably in the 1300s, the Athapaskans separated, a portion beginning a long migration southward. Three hundred years later, Spanish officials would identify several Apache "tribes" surrounding their isolated frontier settlements in present-day New Mexico, for the Apacheans had split into fairly distinct divisions sometime during their epic journey to the Southwest. Fray Alonso de Benavidas, a Franciscan priest, referred to them in 1630 as the "Great Apache Nation." That "nation" included the Chiricahua, Jicarilla, Kiowa Apache, Lipan, Mescalero, Western Apache, and Navajo, but even within these tribes there were further divisions, some tribes being made up of numerous bands, with these bands divided into smaller groups, each with a recognized leader. The vast territory they occupied the Spaniards called *Apachería*.

Geronimo would say that when "Ussen [God] created the Apaches, He also created their homes in the West. He gave them such grain, fruits, and game as they needed to eat. . . . He gave them a pleasant climate and all they needed for clothing and shelter was at hand." Some

Apache cultivated small secluded fields where they raised squash, beans, and corn. Medicinal herbs grew wild, as did a variety of tobacco. But while there were times when the Southwest may have seemed a veritable paradise, the Apache were not destined to have this land all to themselves. Relations with their neighbors, be they Indian or Spaniard, varied greatly. The Apache could be valued allies united against a common threat, or, just as easily, the most bitter of enemies. For most of the seventeenth and eighteenth centuries, except for sporadic periods of peace, Apache groups regularly raided Spanish settlements and Indian pueblos while Spanish presidial soldiers and militia campaigned against the Apache. Both sides sought spoils in these encounters, which, in addition to livestock, included women and children, the basis of a slave trade important to Apache and Spaniard alike.

MEDICINAL SWEET SCENT, CHIRICAHUA MOUNTAINS, ARIZONA

Spanish officials struggled long and hard to end Apache marauding and restrict the several tribes to what were essentially reservations. Lt. José Cortés of the Spanish Royal Corps of Engineers wrote in awe of the Apache in 1799, stating that they displayed their greatest bravery and daring when attacked: "They never lose their composure, even when they are surprised and have no defense at hand. They fight to the last breath, and members of several groups prefer death to surrender."

After winning independence from Spain in 1821, Mexican officials inherited an uneasy northern frontier. Writing in 1844, Santa Fe trader Josiah Gregg observed that the "depredations of the Apaches have been of such long duration, that, beyond the immediate purlieus of the towns, the whole country from New Mexico to the borders of Durango is almost entirely depopulated." Numerous atrocities committed by both sides only served to spawn more vicious reprisals. So desperate did the State of Chihuahua, Mexico, become that for a short time in 1837 it established a reward for Apache scalps: $100 for men, $50 for women, and $25 for children.

It was into this volatile world that an Apache boy named Goyahkla —"He Who Yawns"—was born near the headwaters of the Gila River sometime in the early to mid-1820s.

FOUR IS A SACRED NUMBER

When a child my mother taught me the legends of
our people; taught me of the sun and sky, the moon
and stars, the clouds and storms.

—GERONIMO, 1906

MULE DEER, NEW MEXICO

Geronimo, the name Goyahkla would acquire years later from the Mexicans, was born into a band of the Chiricahua Apache called the Bedonkohe in the early 1820s. The smallest of the Chiricahua bands, they numbered only a few hundred people. In his dictated autobiography, Geronimo would say that he was the fourth-born in a family of four boys and four girls, four being a sacred number for the Chiricahua. Geronimo's father was Taklishim, son of the great Bedonkohe leader Mahko. His mother's name has come down to us as Juana, a Spanish name indicative of the interconnections—through raiding, trading, enslavement, or otherwise—that had developed over time between the Southwest's Hispanic population and the Apache.

In old age, Geronimo recalled his very first years of life: rolling on the earth floor of his father's hide lodge, hanging in a cradle from his mother's back, or, when his mother wanted to work unencumbered, hanging in that same cradle from the branch of a tree. "I was warmed by the sun, rocked by the winds, and sheltered by the trees as other Indian babes." As a young boy, he played games with his brothers and sisters.

ANTELOPE HEADDRESS

Geronimo remembered taking part in "hide and seek" and also pretending with his playmates to be warriors stalking a pretend enemy. His father regaled him with stories of "the brave deeds of our warriors, of the pleasures of the chase, and the glories of the warpath."

Geronimo would get his first taste of "the chase" when he was about eight or ten years of age. The Bedonkohe hunted mule deer, elk, antelope, turkey, and even the bison or buffalo. To find buffalo, however, the Apache hunting parties had to make the long journey to the plains of eastern New Mexico. Geronimo considered deer to be the most difficult prey. Making sure to keep the wind in their faces, Apache hunters could "spend hours in stealing upon grazing deer. If they were in the open we would crawl long distances on the ground, keeping a weed or brush before us, so that our approach would not be noticed." The meat would be dried and stored for up to several months and the skins tanned to a pliable softness for making articles of clothing. "Perhaps no other animal," Geronimo explained, "was more valuable to us than the deer."

The skills Geronimo learned as a young hunter would also serve him well as a warrior. But to become a warrior, one had to go through a rigorous apprenticeship. Geronimo's second cousin, Jason Betzinez, explained that the "way to learn was to go on several raids with an experienced man, taking care of his horses and equipment, standing guard, and cooking his meat for him. That was the Apache custom. . . . As a result of this system our warriors, though never numerous, were extremely capable and resourceful" (Betzinez would one day earn warrior status by serving as Geronimo's apprentice). It was said that an Apache could not be accepted into the "council of warriors" until he had accompanied the warriors four times—again, the sacred number. Geronimo said that he was accepted into the council at age seventeen. "I hoped soon to serve my people in battle," he remembered. "I had long desired to fight with our warriors."

APACHE
BUCKSKIN
BAG

TRAGEDY AT JANOS

[T]he Apache never forgot nor forgave . . .

—JASON BETZINEZ, 1959

BASASEACHIC FALLS IN PARQUE NACIONAL BASASEACHIC, CHIHUAHUA, MEXICO

Taklishim died when Geronimo was still a boy. His wife, Juana, never remarried, choosing instead to live with her young son, Geronimo, who took on the role of provider for his mother. Immediately after Geronimo gained warrior status, he made arrangements to wed a girl he had long been in love with: Alope, a member of another Chiricahua band known as the Nednhi. Geronimo remembered that her father asked many ponies for Alope, but the young man was undeterred. He took a few days to gather the animals and, upon delivering the herd, rode off with Alope. "This was all the marriage ceremony necessary in our tribe," he stated. The Bedonkohe warrior made a new lodge or wigwam near the one for his mother, and, together, he and Alope "followed the traditions of our fathers and were happy." "Three children came to us," Geronimo recalled, "children that played, loitered, and worked as I had done."

This is not to say that Geronimo or the Bedonkohe remained at peace while Geronimo's family grew. His desire to fight as an Apache warrior was easily fulfilled, for the 1840s saw protracted hostilities within certain parts of northern Mexico. Under their able and defiant leader Mangas Coloradas, war parties left the Bedonkohe *rancherías* of what is now New Mexico and Arizona and traveled south, striking terror among the citizens of the Mexican state of Sonora. Yet at the same time, the state adjoining Sonora on the east, Chihuahua, became a Chiricahua refuge of sorts, where the Apache could trade the booty they acquired in neighboring Sonora. In exchange for peaceful relations, Chihuahua had a policy of issuing rations to the Apache. Sonora had no such policy.

According to Betzinez, Chiricahua war parties had "numerous small fights with civilians and soldiers in Sonora, to whom Goyahkla [Geronimo] gradually became well and unfavorably known." In January of 1851, as Geronimo and other Chiricahua under Mangas Coloradas were returning north with over a thousand horses and cattle from a particularly devastating raid, a Mexican force under Capt. Ignacio Pesqueira laid in wait for the Apache at a place called Pozo Hediondo. The Mexican troops, numbering one hundred men, surprised and routed the Apache column's advance contingent, the soldiers excitedly giving chase to the retreating warriors—until they ran straight into the main body of approximately 150 Chiricahua. The resulting clash was the most intense and bloody battle Geronimo had yet experienced, lasting several hours. According to S. M. Barrett, who later took down and edited

Geronimo's recollections, it was at this battle that the Mexicans gave Geronimo (Jerome in English) his now-legendary name. It seems more likely, however, that he acquired his moniker through nonhostile encounters with the Mexicans, either during trade or parleys.

The stunning Mexican defeat at Pozo Hediondo—Captain Pesqueira suffered seventy-two killed and wounded—would have fateful consequences for Geronimo and his people. The commander of Sonora's modest military force, Col. José María Carrasco, determined to punish the Apache in Chihuahua, particularly the Chiricahua who received rations at the town of Janos. These, he suspected, were using Janos as a base to raid into Sonora. "I waited until the allotted time for the Apaches to visit Janos to obtain their regular rations," Carrasco later explained, and "by forced marches at night succeeded in reaching the place just as the carnival was at its height." Carrasco's surprise attack was decisive and deadly, his 400-man force killing at least 21 Apache outright and taking 62 prisoners, mostly women and children. The Mexican colonel would subsequently boast that his men had killed 130.

Among those killed by Carrasco's Sonorans were Geronimo's wife, Alope, his three children, and his mother, Juana. Geronimo would claim that the Mexican soldiers had gotten the Apache hopelessly drunk before murdering them. Jason Betzinez, on the other hand, states that Geronimo and other warriors were in the town drinking while the attack was made on the nearby rancherías. In any event, upon Geronimo's return to his home village, probably in New Mexico, he had to face the decorations Alope had made for their lodge and the stray toys of their children. "I burned them all, even our tipi. I also burned my mother's tipi and destroyed all her property."

Years later, when Geronimo related this tragic chapter in his life to artist E. A. Burbank, the artist recalled that the aged warrior became extremely agitated. "He rose from his bed, his dark face almost white with anger as he shook his fist in my face, fairly hissing, as he declared, 'After that I killed every white man I saw.'"

WHITE EYES

As enemies, the Mexicans were nothing in
comparison with the White Eyes who
came in from the east.

—ASA DAKLUGIE, CIRCA EARLY 1950S

CAVE CREEK IN THE CHIRICAHUA MOUNTAINS, ARIZONA

Geronimo's own story of his life after the massacre of his family is a recounting of one raid into Mexico after another. At times he would set off on foot with as few as two fellow warriors; at others the raiding party could number as many as twenty-five. Before departing on a large raid, careful preparations were made for the safety of the women, children, and elderly left behind. Usually, the camp would break apart and scatter in different directions, reassembling at a predetermined location many miles away. "In this way it would be hard for the Mexicans to trail them and we would know where to find our families when we returned," Geronimo said. Additionally, if any tribes hostile to the Chiricahua happened to observe the raiding party leaving the area, they would fail to locate the vulnerable ranchería.

CHIRICAHUA NATIONAL MONUMENT, ARIZONA

Geronimo claimed to be the leader of many of these forays, and although he spoke of them as motivated by his desire for revenge, it is also true that Apache subsistence relied to a great extent on livestock and other plunder stolen from Mexican ranchers and Indian farmers. Warriors and tribal leaders attained that status by proving themselves on raids, Apache women greeting successful raiders with "songs and rejoicing."

Regardless of their actual motivation, however, what is clear from Geronimo's reminiscences is that these raids almost always had bloody results, for both sides. The Apache dealt death without remorse, as did their enemies. In Apachería, violence and tragedy were always lurking.

Another player entered the world of the Chiricahua with the signing of the Treaty of Guadalupe Hidalgo between the United States and Mexico in February of 1848. This treaty ended the U.S.–Mexican War and transferred to the United States much of the present-day Southwest, including California, where gold had been discovered just a little over a week before the treaty was signed. When news of this discovery reached the States, the rush began, bringing thousands of gold hunters overland, a good portion through Apachería. In 1854, in what was known as the Gadsden Purchase, the United States acquired from Mexico an additional twenty-nine million acres in present-day Arizona and New Mexico. This purchase embraced the heart of Chiricahua territory, including the Chiricahua Mountains, from which the famed Apache tribe received its name.

LT. GEORGE BASCOM

Originally secured for a proposed railroad route, the Gadsden Purchase contained an important communication and travel corridor connecting California and New Mexico. In 1856, the U.S. military began a long presence in the area with the establishment of Fort Buchanan twenty-five miles east of the Hispanic settlement of Tubac. The post's mission was to guard against Apache threats in the region—a region beginning to see more and more Anglos, particularly miners—and to keep the travel routes open. That mission became weightier the following year with the start of a regular stage line between San Antonio and San Diego and then the inauguration in 1858 of the famed Butterfield Overland Mail. Stretching from St. Louis to San Francisco, the line required numerous relay stations, one of which was located in the heart of Apache Pass, an often dreaded gauntlet separating the Dos Cabezas Mountains on the north from the Chiricahua Mountains on the south.

The Chiricahua maintained friendly relations during this period with their government-appointed Indian agents and also employees of the Butterfield Overland Mail. In fact, the Chokonen band of

Chiricahua under Cochise, the son-in-law of Mangas Coloradas, is said to have had an arrangement to provide some of the Butterfield's stage stations with firewood. Yet tensions rose steadily as Apache raiding—on both sides of the border—continued, and conflicts with miners and ranchers became more frequent. Those tensions exploded at Siphon Canyon (200 yards east of the Apache Pass stage station) on February 4, 1861, when Lt. George Bascom attempted to capture Cochise. Bascom hoped to secure the release of a boy recently seized in a raid near Fort Buchanan, but the lieutenant made a terrible blunder, for Cochise's people were not the culprits. And Bascom underestimated the ferocity of the Chiricahua leader, who escaped in the midst of their parley by slashing through the officer's tent with his knife and making a mad dash to safety.

Some of Cochise's band who had accompanied him to Siphon Canyon were unable to flee with their chief, and Bascom held them as bargaining chips. Cochise immediately set about gathering his own hostages, attacking anyone unfortunate enough to be traveling through Apache Pass, but, in the end, there would be no exchange. Cochise executed his prisoners and Lt. Isaiah Moore, who had assumed command of the troops in Apache Pass, hanged six Apache warriors in his possession. The tragic "Cut Through the Tent" affair, as it came to be known by the Apache (the "Bascom Affair" to whites), resulted in all-out war. "After this trouble all of the Indians agreed not to be friendly with the white men any more," Geronimo remembered. "There was no general engagement, but a long struggle followed. Sometimes we attacked the white men—sometimes they attacked us."

Geronimo is not believed to have participated in the events of February 1861, but he apparently was involved in a surprise attack on a detachment of California Volunteers marching eastward through Apache Pass on July fifteenth of the following year. Led by Cochise and Mangas Coloradas, some 110 to 120 Apache warriors opened fire on the soldiers from stone breastworks overlooking the abandoned stage station and the nearby Apache Spring. The Chiricahua, however, were no match for the Californians' two howitzers, and the Apache soon fled from the artillery fire. A second fight with the same result occurred the next day, after which the Chiricahua abandoned the important spring to the soldiers. This "Battle of Apache Pass" resulted in the establishment of Fort Bowie near the spring, a post that would have a fateful place in Geronimo's life.

Six months after the Battle of Apache Pass, a chance for peace with the Chiricahua under Mangas Coloradas was irretrievably lost through the treachery of White Eyes (the Chiricahua name for white Americans). Mangas had taken half of his people to the mining settlement of Pinos Altos, New Mexico Territory, on the assurances of the whites there that the Apache could live near them in peace and receive government rations. Instead, the trusting chief was led into a trap, taken prisoner, and subsequently turned over to the U.S. Army at Fort McLane. In the early morning hours of January 19, 1863, Mangas was murdered by his guards "while trying to escape." The great chief was later scalped and decapitated, his head boiled to obtain its skull. It was, Geronimo would later say about the grisly episode, "perhaps the greatest wrong ever done to the Indians."

USSEN'S PROMISE

We know there is a God who
can protect us even against a thousand.

—JAMES KAYWAYKLA, 1956

Unlike Mangas, Geronimo had been unwilling to trust the Americans. He claimed that Mangas left him in charge of the Bedonkohe who remained behind in what is now Arizona, where they waited anxiously for news regarding their leader's peace overtures. "No word ever came to us from them," Geronimo said. Mangas's murder, and the U.S. Army's subsequent attacks on the Chiricahua, left Geronimo's group vulnerable, for they had sent most of their arms and ammunition with Mangas. Short on provisions, they retreated to the Apache Pass area. Here the Apache warriors came upon four men driving a herd of cattle. Quickly killing the men, Geronimo's group drove the cattle into the mountains, but they were interrupted in their butchering work by a surprise attack from a column of cavalry. Despite his people's usual tactic of scattering and reassembling at a safe place miles away, Geronimo tells us that these same troopers located and attacked their ranchería again ten days later. After a day of fighting, the Chiricahua fled farther into the mountains.

Without adequate provisions and arms, and weakened in numbers, Mangas's Bedonkohe band of Chiricahua broke apart, never to reassemble. The surviving Bedonkohe joined the other three Chiricahua bands: the Chokonen under Cochise, the Chihenne under Victorio, and the Nednhi under Juh. Juh, whose name meant "Long Neck," had married a cousin of Geronimo's, and it was Juh's Nednhi that Geronimo joined. For the next several years, though, hardly anything is known of Geronimo's activities. Jason Betzinez would write that Juh and his band spent most of their "time preying on the Mexicans and hiding in the almost inaccessible mountains of northern Chihuahua and Sonora." Geronimo, too, stated that the Nednhi's lands "extended far into Mexico." "Their Chief, Whoa [Juh], was a brother to me," Geronimo recalled, "and we spent much of our time in his territory."

Information regarding Geronimo's family life at this time is sketchy as well. Sometime in the 1850s he took another wife, Chee-hash-kish, also a Bedonkohe, who bore him a son (Chappo) and daughter (Dohn-say). Polygamy being an accepted practice among the Apache, Geronimo married another Bedonkohe woman shortly thereafter named Nana-tha-thtith; she had one child by Geronimo whose name is not recorded. If it was actually possible for Geronimo to harbor a deeper hatred for the Mexican people, he reached that dark place when an attack by Mexican troops on a Chiricahua ranchería left Nana-tha-thtith and their child dead (as well as several other women and children and some warriors).

In the early 1860s, perhaps after Geronimo joined Juh's band, he married She-gha, a Nednhi, and then a Bedonkohe woman named Shtsha-she. Geronimo told S. M. Barrett that he "might have had as many wives as he wished, but he. . . . was so busy fighting Mexicans that he could not support more than two." Despite this statement by Geronimo, there were times when the warrior's wives apparently numbered as many as three.

A story strong in Apache lore centers around Juh's wife, Ishton (the cousin with whom Geronimo was very close), and the difficult delivery of her baby, Asa Daklugie, about 1869–70. Geronimo was present at the childbirth as medicine man, the earliest reference we have to Geronimo's much-lauded powers. But, according to Daklugie himself, his mother's labor went on for four excruciating days. "Geronimo thought that she was going to die," Daklugie said, "he had done all he could for her, and was so distressed that he climbed high up the mountain behind Fort Bowie to plead with Ussen for. . . . [Ishton's] life." Geronimo raised his arms and eyes to the sky and then heard Ussen's voice. "Ussen told Geronimo that . . . [Ishton] was to live, and he promised my uncle that he would never be killed but would live to a ripe old age and would die a natural death."

It was Ussen's promise to Geronimo, Daklugie believed, that made Geronimo so fearless. "He was by nature already a brave person," Daklugie recalled, "but if one knows he will never be killed, why be afraid?" Indeed, decades later, Geronimo would tell artist E. A. Burbank: "Bullets cannot kill me!" Geronimo would never be a chief of the Chiricahua, a point that was often confused even during Geronimo's lifetime, but his powers as medicine man demanded great respect and, at times, fear. It gave him tremendous influence that, combined with his prowess as a warrior, allowed him to later assume leadership of whatever Chiricahua band or group he was associated with. "In times of danger," stated Jason Betzinez, "he was the man to be relied upon."

RESERVATION & IMPRISONMENT

I have seen many looks of hate in my
long life, but never one so vicious, so vengeful.

—APACHE AGENT JOHN CLUM,
AFTER TAKING GERONIMO'S RIFLE, 1877

WINTER STORM, DRAGOON MOUNTAINS, ARIZONA

 AT SAN CARLOS, AGENT CLUM POSES WITH DIABLO (LEFT) AND ESKIMINZIN

APACHE PRISONERS OF WAR

In late April and early May of 1871, a detachment of eighteen men under Lt. Howard B. Cushing—one of the Army's more successful Indian fighters—scouted southern Arizona hoping to capture Cochise and his followers. But in the Whetstone Mountains, Cushing ran into Juh's band, which, many believe, included Geronimo as well. According to Juh's son, Asa Daklugie, the chief "had heard much about this Lieutenant Cushing and his depredations in Arizona . . . [and] was determined to kill that man." Decoyed into a trap, Cushing and two of his men were killed. Juh lost as many as thirteen men in the fight, but Daklugie would say that it was the "engagement in which Juh took the greatest pride."

Frustrated in its efforts to defeat Cochise, the Army entered into a peace agreement with the Chiricahua leader at a camp in the Dragoon Mountains in October of 1872. Geronimo's dictated memoirs suggest that he took part in this famed meeting between Cochise and Gen. Oliver Otis Howard, but Geronimo makes no mention of Cochise and claims instead to have personally made a treaty with Howard at Fort Bowie. While some scholars doubt Geronimo's presence at the negotiations, Geronimo and Juh soon brought their people to the new reservation established by the 1872 treaty, a reservation that incorporated much of the traditional Chiricahua homeland. "When beef was issued to the Indians I got twelve steers for my tribe," Geronimo recalled, "and Cochise got twelve steers for his tribe." The rations were issued about once a month.

Although Cochise kept most of the Chiricahua at peace in southeastern Arizona, he did nothing, initially, to prevent raiding across the border into Mexico. In July of 1873, for example, Chiricahua Indian agent Tom Jeffords confiscated a Mexican boy from Geronimo; the boy had been taken captive the month previous at Concepción, Chihuahua. With Cochise's death in 1874, the Apache lost another strong leader and shrewd negotiator for his people. The Chiricahua would receive an equally devastating blow a short time later, for the Indian Department was determined to concentrate the various Apache tribes together on one reservation far from the troublesome border. Consequently, on October 30, 1876, President Ulysses S. Grant revoked the Chiricahua reservation Cochise had won four years earlier. Cochise's eldest son and successor, Taza, and 325 Chiricahua were moved to the San Carlos Reservation, a place Jason Betzinez described as "worthless to whites and Indians alike."

Geronimo and Juh, however, escaped to their old haunts in Sonora.

Living away from the reservation meant no more government beef rations. Survival for these maverick Apache forced a return to raiding—raiding for weapons, ammunition, horses, and other livestock. At the beginning of January 1877, a band of Chiricahua under Geronimo's leadership raided a ranch east of Tubac, Arizona. A Fort Bowie cavalry detachment of fifty-two men (including thirty-four Apache scouts) under Lt. John A. Rucker quickly struck the trail of the raiders and their herd of stolen horses, following it to present-day Lordsburg, New Mexico, where the trail turned south, leading Rucker and his men through the Pyramid Mountains and to the Animas Mountains beyond. Their dogged pursuit climaxed with the surprise of Geronimo's ranchería on January 9. The fierce two-hour battle that followed ended with the Chiricahua fleeing; Geronimo suffered ten dead and a number wounded. The Chiricahua had not been handed such a harsh blow from the U.S. military in years. Curiously, Geronimo makes no mention of this defeat in his reminiscences.

Two months later, Geronimo and approximately one hundred followers—with some one hundred stolen horses—appeared at the Ojo Caliente Reservation in New Mexico, home to Victorio's Chihenne band. Much to his displeasure, Geronimo was denied rations for the time he had been off the reservation, time spent raiding in Arizona and New Mexico. With Geronimo's whereabouts now known, orders came from Washington, D.C., for his arrest and removal to San Carlos. That formidable job fell to Agent John Clum, who arrived at Ojo Caliente on April 20. The next day, while most of his command of 102 Indian police hid from view in the Indian agency's commissary building, Clum sent a messenger to Geronimo's camp asking for a conference. The unsuspecting warrior and his men defiantly entered Clum's trap. When Clum informed Geronimo of his orders, Geronimo bristled, telling the agent: "We are not going to San Carlos with you, and unless you are very careful, you and your Apache police will not go back to San Carlos, either." Clum abruptly marched out his hidden reserves, however, and then disarmed the confounded Chiricahua leader. Geronimo and six others, now branded "renegade" Apache, were put in chains and placed under guard. They and their people—along with Victorio's Chihenne (often referred to as the Warm Springs Apache)—would indeed be removed to San Carlos, an overland march that would take them twenty days to complete.

Clum's orders stated that the "renegades" were to be held in confinement at San Carlos for "murder and robbery," and the agent was prepared to turn Geronimo and his other Apache prisoners over to the Pima County sheriff in Tucson for trial. Fortunately for Geronimo, Clum resigned his position in July of 1877, and shortly thereafter, Clum's successor, H. L. Hart, ordered Geronimo released from the guardhouse. Years later, John Clum would tell acquaintances that he "should have hung Geronimo over at Hot Springs and never bothered about bringing him to San Carlos."

——— ✦ ———

THE BEGINNING OF THE END

The Odds were only five hundred to one against
Geronimo, but still they could not whip him nor could
they capture him.

—ASA DAKLUGIE, CIRCA EARLY 1950S

CANDY BARREL CACTUS AND CLIFFROSE, FOOTHILLS OF THE SIERRA MADRE, MEXICO

Geronimo would say that while all went well at San Carlos after his release, "we were not satisfied." The policy of placing several different Apache tribes together on one reservation might have seemed logical and economical to whites in Washington, D.C., but the various Apache groups were not always on the best of terms. Also, instances of smallpox and malaria, plus inadequate rations, led to considerable unrest and, eventually, the breakout of many Chiricahua. Although Geronimo initially promised Agent Hart that he would not flee the reservation, he broke that pledge on August 2, 1878. According to Jason Betzinez, Geronimo started south with his family after a nephew committed suicide. Geronimo had scolded the young man during a drinking spree and blamed himself for his nephew's death. The acting Indian agent, however, reported that Geronimo fled because he realized the incident would lead to the revelation that his band had been making *tizwin* (an undistilled corn liquor), and he "was afraid of being put in the guardhouse." "From a hideout in the Sierra Madres," wrote Betzinez, Geronimo and Juh "resumed their raids into Sonora."

A year later, Victorio and his band broke out from San Carlos and commenced raiding and killing. Despite the close ties between Victorio's people and those of Juh and Geronimo, however, the two groups did not join forces. In fact, Juh and Geronimo sent peace overtures to the military in the fall of 1879 and returned to reservation life at San Carlos the following December or January.

Calling it a "surrender," Tucson's *Arizona Star* commented that "These Indians belong to Cachise's [sic] old tribe—the worst in the deck." San Carlos had not gotten any better—"the place was almost uninhabitable," remembered Betzinez—but somehow Geronimo managed to settle down for over a year. In the spring of 1881, though, an Apache mystic named Noch-ay-del-klinne caused a fervor among both Apache and whites with wild prophecies that promised the disappearance of White Eyes. The killing of the prophet in a melee with U.S. troops on Cibecue Creek in August only heightened tensions.

A "rumor was current that the officers were again planning to imprison our leaders," remembered Geronimo. "This rumor served to revive the memory of all our past wrongs." When the military requested Geronimo's presence for a conference at Fort Thomas, the warrior feared treachery. "We thought it more manly to die on the warpath than to be killed in prison." At the end of September 1881, then, Geronimo and Juh with 250 followers again sought refuge in Mexico. Mexico, however, was becoming less and less a refuge for the Apache. According to Geronimo, the "Mexicans were gathering troops in the mountains where we had been ranging, and their numbers were so much greater than ours that we could not hope to fight them successfully, and we were tired of being chased about from place to place."

Juh and Geronimo devised a bold plan to bolster their forces. In the spring of 1882, they conducted a daring raid on San Carlos, where they forced the remnants of Victorio's Warm Springs Apache, now under Chief Loco (Victorio had been killed by a Mexican militia in 1880) to accompany them back to Mexico. Betzinez and his family were among

GERONIMO AND GENERAL CROOK IN SURRENDER NEGOTIATIONS AT CAÑON DE LOS EMBUDOS IN MEXICO.

those Warm Springs Apache taken from San Carlos. "It now began to be clear to me," he observed during the dangerous flight south, "that Geronimo was pretty much the main leader although he was not the born chief of any band. . . . But Geronimo seemed to be the most intelligent and resourceful as well as the most vigorous and farsighted." After hard skirmishes with both U.S. and Mexican troops, and severe losses for the renegades, the Chiricahua reached Juh's camp "deep in the almost inaccessible Sierra Madres."

With the Sierra Madres as a base, the renegade or "Wild Indians," numbering several hundred according to Betzinez, made long forays afield. When Geronimo slipped across the border into Arizona and New Mexico, it was to acquire much-needed ammunition. Every raid risked detection, and as the military was using skilled Apache Indian scouts, detection meant there was a good chance of a fight. "I do not think that he wanted to kill," recalled Charlie Smith, a young member of Geronimo's band. "If he were seen by a civilian, it meant that he would be reported to the military and they'd be after us. So there was nothing to do but kill the civilian and his entire family. It was terrible to see little children killed. . . . There were times that I hated Geronimo for that, too; but when I got older, I knew that he had no choice." Not all of these killings were committed by Geronimo's people, however, for there were other Apache raiders then at large.

MAJ. GEN. GEORGE CROOK

While Geronimo was a fearless warrior and powerful medicine man, Jason Betzinez tells us he had a weakness for liquor, and it was Geronimo's desire for mescal that led him to make contact with the people of Casas Grandes, Chihuahua. "We shook hands . . . and began to trade, and the Mexicans gave us mescal," Geronimo remembered. "Soon nearly all the Indians were drunk. While they were drunk two companies of Mexican troops, from another town, attacked us. . . . We fled in all directions." As many as twelve warriors were killed and over two dozen women and children captured. Among those captured was Chee-hash-kish, Geronimo's wife—they would never see each other again. Soon Geronimo would take another wife: Zi-yeh, a Nednhi.

Geronimo's people suffered another setback in May of 1883 when their ranchería was discovered and captured by a U.S. expeditionary force under Gen. George Crook while Geronimo and his warriors were away. Crook, commander of the Department of Arizona, had crossed the international border with 244 fighting men, over three-quarters of whom were Apache

NEAR THE SUMMIT OF MT. PEÑA NEVADA, SIERRA MADRE, MEXICO

scouts. Geronimo arrived at the ranchería five days after its capture, and following several conferences with Crook, he agreed to return to San Carlos. Geronimo did not return to U.S. territory, however, until February of 1884, arriving at the agency with nine warriors and twenty-two noncombatants (Juh had died the previous November). Bringing up the rear was a herd of some 135 cattle. Much to Geronimo's displeasure, Crook confiscated the stock. Geronimo's plea that "these were not white men's cattle, but belonged to us, for we had taken them from the Mexicans during our wars" could only have strengthened the general's resolve (the cattle were subsequently sold and the proceeds sent to Mexico).

SURRENDER & CELEBRITY

He was one of the brightest, most resolute, determined looking men that I have ever encountered. He had the clearest, sharpest, dark eye I think I have ever seen, unless it was that of General Sherman. . . . Every movement indicated power, energy and determination. In everything he did he had a purpose.

—MAJ. GEN. NELSON A. MILES, 1896

As in the past, all seemed well at San Carlos, but in May of 1885, again fearing military reprisals for making tizwin and getting intoxicated, Geronimo led 134 Chiricahua in a race for the Mexican border. With Geronimo was Naiche, the second son of Cochise and the hereditary chief of the Chiricahua after Taza's death from pneumonia in 1876. Eluding their pursuers, and killing and raiding as they went, the renegades once again escaped to Mexico. Geronimo became the most wanted —and feared—man in both countries, with the U.S. Army marshaling all its resources to find and capture the outlaws, regardless of which side of the border they were on.

Finally, in January of 1886, Crook's Apache scouts discovered the remote Chiricahua camp. Geronimo and his followers escaped capture, but they lost nearly everything in the ranchería to Crook's soldiers, including their horses and precious supplies. Geronimo was now ready to talk surrender terms with the general. They met for three days beginning March 25 at Cañon de los Embudos, just south of the international boundary. Tucson photographer C. S. Fly took an amazing series of photographs of the defiant Apache and their meeting with Crook.

On the third day of the negotiations, Geronimo agreed to return with Crook's force. "Once I moved about like the wind," Geronimo told the general. "Now I surrender to you and that is all." Geronimo shook hands with Crook but the Chiricahua was not to honor his pledge. A trader named Tribolet supplied Geronimo and others with liquor, and the drinking began. Again, paranoia set in regarding their eventual treatment. Geronimo's followers started on the long march to San Carlos on the twenty-eighth, with certain of the Chiricahua continuing to partake of Tribolet's alcohol. That night, Geronimo, Naiche, and forty-five others slipped out of the camp. The hunt for the renegade began all over again, but now with Nelson A. Miles in charge of the Department of Arizona (Crook asked to be relieved in the wake of harsh criticism regarding Geronimo's escape).

The final surrender came a little over six months later on September 4, 1886, in a place called Skeleton Canyon, within the Peloncillo Range of Arizona and New Mexico. Those Chiricahua who had months earlier accompanied Crook to San Carlos had been shipped to exile in Florida, and now Miles promised Geronimo and his warriors that they would be reunited with their relatives and friends in Florida in five days. Geronimo firmly believed Miles made another promise that day as well, one assuring him that the Chiricahua would eventually have their own reservation with "plenty of timber, water, and grass." In old age, Geronimo would relate how he "looked in vain for General Miles to send me to that land of which he had spoken; I longed in vain for the implements, house, and stock that General Miles had promised me."

To the outrage of most of the white citizens of Arizona, who wanted Geronimo and his renegades hanged, Geronimo, Naiche, and their small band departed Bowie Station under military guard on September 8. They did not join their relatives, however, nor were the warriors allowed to be with their immediate families. Instead, Geronimo and his men were sent to Fort Pickens, Florida, the women and children joining the other Chiricahua captives already at Fort Marion. In April of 1887, the families of the Fort Pickens prisoners were brought to the island compound. The following year, all of the Chiricahua were congregated at Mount Vernon Barracks, Alabama. "We were not healthy in this place," Geronimo said, "for the climate disagreed with us." In fact, an alarming number of Chiricahua had perished due to the unhealthy conditions of their living arrangements in both Florida and Alabama. Then, in the fall of 1894, the Chiricahua were moved once again, this time to Fort Sill, Oklahoma.

As the years passed, Geronimo came to be much in demand for public appearances, particularly at national expositions and Wild West shows. He was one of the featured attractions at the St. Louis World's Fair in 1904, where he sold photographs, autographs, and bows and arrows, making more money "than I have ever owned before." In 1905 he upstaged President Theodore Roosevelt at his inaugural parade in Washington, D.C., the sight of the old warrior on horseback drawing forth cheers and shouts. In a meeting with Roosevelt a few days later, however, Geronimo was in tears as he begged for the return of his Chiricahua to the Southwest. "Please, please take the rope

GERONIMO (TOP HAT)
IN OKLAHOMA

from the hands of me and my people and let us be free," he pleaded. "We are tired of living in a strange land and want to go back to our old home. We will be good." Roosevelt refused.

Geronimo lived out the rest of his years a prisoner of war at Fort Sill, where the soldiers got to calling him "Gerry," a nickname the once fearsome warrior detested. He enjoyed gambling, horse racing, and, not surprisingly, drinking. On the night of February 11, 1909, drunk from whiskey, Geronimo fell from his horse and remained prostrate for the rest of the winter night. He contracted pneumonia from this exposure and died at the post hospital on February seventeenth. He was approximately eighty-six years old.

Asa Daklugie recalled his uncle's death: "We could not burn his house; and, though he had not died in it, that should have been done out of respect. We could not bury his best war horse with him, but I saw that he had it for the journey. We placed his most treasured possessions in his grave. . . . He walks through eternity garbed as a chief in his ceremonial robes and his medicine hat. He rides a fine horse. He has his best weapons."

In 1913 the Chiricahua were allowed to return to their beloved home-land. Nearly two-hundred moved to New Mexico's Mescalero Apache Reservation, while the remaining Chiricahua kept their homes in Oklahoma, the final resting place of Geronimo's bones.

FURTHER READING

Ball, Eve, with Nora Henn and Lynda A. Sanchez. *Indeh: An Apache Odyssey.* Norman: University of Oklahoma Press, 1988.

Barrett, S. M., ed. *Geronimo's Story of His Life.* 1906. Reprint. New York: Meridian, 1996.

Betzinez, Jason, with W. S. Nye. *I Fought with Geronimo.* Harrisburg, Pennsylvania: The Stackpole Company, 1959.

Cortés, José. *Views from the Apache Frontier: Report on the Northern Provinces of New Spain.* Edited by Elizabeth A. H. John. Norman: University of Oklahoma Press, 1989.

Debo, Angie. *Geronimo: The Man, His Time, His Place.* Norman: University of Oklahoma Press, 1976.

Kraft, Louis. *Gatewood & Geronimo.* Albuquerque: University of New Mexico Press, 2000.

Miles, Nelson A. *Personal Recollections & Observations of Nelson A. Miles.* 1896. Reprint. Lincoln: University of Nebraska Press, 1992.

Roberts, David. *They Moved Like the Wind: Cochise, Geronimo and the Apache Wars.* New York: Simon & Schuster, 1993.

Robinson, Sherry. *Apache Voices: Their Stories of Survival as Told to Eve Ball.* Albuquerque: University of New Mexico Press, 2000.

Sweeney, Edwin R. *Cochise: Chiricahua Apache Chief.* Norman: University of Oklahoma Press, 1991.

———. *Mangas Coloradas: Chief of the Chiricahua Apaches.* Norman: University of Oklahoma Press, 1998.